MW01058401

How <u>NOT</u> To Make A PRIZE-WINNING QUILT

By Ami Simms

All the quilts pictured in this book are ones I have made with my own hands. I stress this point for two reasons: first it isn't nice to take other people's work and make fun of it, and second I want to make sure it is clearly understood that I made these quilts with my own hands and not with my *feet!*

I present *"How Not To Make A Prize-Winning Quilt"* because it's healthy for everyone, quiltmakers included, to laugh at themselves every now and again. Feel free to use my quilts to get you going. And it's important for beginning quilters to realize that very few people start out making perfect quilts. This does not in the least diminish the pleasure we can derive from our efforts, even the most humble ones.

Mallery Press ◆ 4206 Sheraton Dr. ◆ Flint, Michigan 48532 USA
1-800-A-STITCH

First Edition.
How Not To Make A Prize-Winning Quilt. Copyright ©1994 by Ami Simms. Printed and bound in the United States of America. ALL RIGHTS RESERVED. No part of this book may be reproduced or transmitted in any form, or by any means, including, but not limited to, photocopying, recording, or by any informational storage or retrieval system without written permission from the publisher, except by a reviewer who may quote brief passages in a review.

Library of Congress Cataloging-In-Publication Data
Simms, Ami, 1954-
    How NOT to make a prize winning quilt / Ami Simms. -- 1st ed.
        p.   cm.
    ISBN: 0-943079-05-5
    1. Quilting.   2. Quilting--Humor.   I. Title.
TT835.S537   1994   94-20438
    746.46--dc20   CIP

Cartoons and front cover design by Jean Pajot Smith.

Contents

Preface

My first quilt show was a real eye-opener. I'd made a handful of quilts but I guess I was no expert. Watching the ladies handling the quilts with white gloves, I thought they all had some kind of communicable skin disease. My friend and I had made the pilgrimage to Ft. Wayne, Indiana, for the 11th Annual National Quilting Association Show. I had taught her everything I knew about quilting the week before, and we decided to go and hobnob with the other quilters.

The instant we walked into the show I knew we were out of their league. In fact, I was sure we weren't even playing the same game. We loved every quilt we saw and couldn't for the life of us figure out why they all weren't wearing ribbons.

After about an hour we risked catching whatever the poor women in the white gloves were afflicted with and asked one to explain how the quilts had been judged. She shared some of the finer points of quilt judging, of which we were totally ignorant. She explained that stitches should be small and even, seams flat, corners square, and bindings fully stuffed. She continued with admonitions against loose stitches, crooked quilting, inconsistent grainline, and non-matching thread. Then she started in on points that don't meet, seams that are pressed to the "light" instead of to the "dark," sloppy miters, and wobbly borders.

If you've ever seen the plastic doggies that sit on the back window ledges of cars and bob their heads up and down as they go down the road, then you'll know exactly what we looked like. The more she explained, the less we understood. Our eyes glazed over and we nodded our heads like plastic doggies. We thanked her and tried to extricate ourselves as she was getting into a long discourse on how it was preferable to have two evenly spaced seams on the back of a quilt instead of one ugly one running right down the middle. (Heaven forbid!) We agreed enthusiastically, smiled, and waved good-bye.

Thankfully, we made it behind the first full-size quilt out of earshot before doubling over with laughter. Maybe the gloves indicated some mental condition: Chronic Picky-itis.

We continued with the rest of the show, admiring the quilts and wondering how the poor souls who entered them would react to learning that the judges were delusional. I figured those gals in the white gloves were also a few inches short of a yard! It was either that, or I was an expert in how not to make a prize-winning quilt. Ah-ha.

Introduction

By the time I tried quilting I had dabbled in just about everything crafty. Coming from a long line of needlewomen I learned how to play with my hands at an early age. My great-grandmother crocheted about a kazillion afghans. She also made lace, knitted entire suits, and embroidered tablecloths and matching napkins with real waste canvas. She made clothes for everyone in the family right down to, and including, the underwear.

My mother sewed all of my clothes until I was 12 and she played with clay on the side. We had a potting wheel and kiln in the basement, and my dad mixed the glazes until he realized some of them were slightly radioactive. (Evidently uranium makes a swell yellow.)

I pinched coils of clay into ashtrays and threw pots on a kick-wheel all through grade school. Knitting, crocheting, macramé, and dressmaking followed in high school. By the time I was a junior in college I had added broom-making, candle-dipping, tin-smithing, jewelry-making, and black-smithing to the list.

I tried all this stuff, but wasn't very good at any of it. My pots blew up in the kiln, my knitting unraveled halfway through, and my crocheted projects were always triangular in shape. The only macramé knot I ever truly mastered was the unintentional variety, and I never could seem to get the hang of following a pattern.

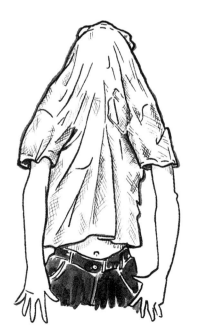

My downfall, it appears, was that I was always looking for a way to speed things up. I once made a T-shirt and figured I could save lots of time by stay-stitching the front and back necks at the same time. It was only after attempting to try it on that I realized I had sewn the head hole shut!

I eventually lost interest in just about everything I tried. Usually this occurred just after I had sunk a small fortune into supplies but before I ever reached that magic moment where one is "ahead of the game."

This mythical state of "ahead" occurs when you actually *can* make whatever it is yourself for less money than just buying one. This, of course, does not include your time.

Losing interest can be a blessing. I discovered early on that broommaking, for example, isn't all it's cracked up to be. There's only one thing I can think of to do with a broom once you've made one and that's the same thing you do with the store-bought variety. If that's not bad enough, you still have to go out and buy the dust pan! I also found that *one* homemade tin candle holder with an honest-to-goodness hand dipped candle was actually *better* than two. They don't improve with age, either.

Jewelry-making got to be too expensive, especially when I used up the last of mother's sterling tea spoons ground up by the garbage disposal and had to purchase my own silver. I was never a very good blacksmith. My horseshoes needed arch supports. I could make a decent fire poker, but students living in dorm rooms have just about as much use for a fire poker as a set of orthopedic horseshoes.

I got into quilting by accident. As luck would have it, I attended a small liberal arts college that still required students to write a thesis in order to graduate. With a major in anthropology it was logical for me to study a foreign culture. Too cheap to leave the country, I chose the Amish. I still don't know why. I had never met an Amish person, but this didn't seem to be a problem.

I hit the library for several weeks, soaked up as much historical information as possible, and determined that the best way to learn about the Amish was to hang out with some and do what they do. In anthro-speak this is referred to as Participant Observation. I'd dress Amish, eat Amish, speak Amish—I'd be the next George Plimpton. All I needed was a family to take me in.

My faculty advisor knew an Old Order Amish family in northern Indiana and wrote me a letter of introduction. If they liked me they would invite me to live with them for six months and my worries would be over. I would smile a lot and be as agreeable as possible.

I learned of a barn raising and showed up unannounced, letter in hand, smiling like an idiot. I handed my letter to Harry Stutzman, my Amish "contact," who gave me the grand tour of the barn. He patiently answered *all* of my questions, even the stupid ones. These were considerable as I was a 19-year-old college kid from the suburbs trying to grasp a devoutly religious and decidedly rural lifestyle with no electricity, automobiles, or designer jeans. After we toured the barn he suggested I go over and meet his wife, Ida, who was at a quilting.

By this time I was smiling so hard my ears hurt. I was grateful for the change in venue so that I could rest my facial muscles on the drive over. Besides, I had heard of quilting bees (something pioneers did in my sixth-grade history book) and we actually had two quilts at home. They were made by a woman who worked for my mother—out of recycled pajamas and boxer shorts. Finally something familiar.

Again I showed up unannounced, but eager to please. I was let into the house and followed the woman to a room in the back. There I was smiling broadly, and there they were—a dozen Old Order Amish women sitting around what appeared to be a large trampoline.

They told me I was staring at a quilt stretched on a quilting frame. By the end of the day most of it would be quilted. They invited me to sit down and join them.

Quilting, they explained, was a simple running stitch. They looked at me as if my mother had taught me that one already. I wanted to mention the clay ashtrays, the knotted macramé, and the fire pokers, but didn't have the nerve.

The Amish women sat around the frame in their plain-colored dresses, their hair drawn up under white prayer coverings. Each had one hand under the quilt and the other on top making perfect stitches. The quilt jumped a little with each tug of the thread and they slid spools and scissors to each other across the top of the quilt with passes Wayne Gretzky would envy.

Offering me a threaded needle, they asked if I wanted to give it a try. Remember my state of mind. I wanted them to like me. A lot. If they didn't like me and invite me to live with them I was back in the library for the next six months. If they had said, "Would you like to take off all your clothes and run naked in the woods?" I probably would have said, "Sure. Sounds good to me!"

They also offered me a thimble. When I told them I didn't need one, they giggled. Undaunted, I watched as experienced fingers maneuvered needles in and out of the fabric sandwich. I imitated them as best I could. After removing the needle from the middle finger of my underneath hand, I was able to bring the needle back up to complete my first stitch.

For those readers not familiar with the term "toe-hooker," this is a stitch so long that if the quilt were ever put on a bed, conceivably one could get one's toe hooked through it. Sadly, I was not even able to make "toe-hookers." I made "foot-hookers." After only a few stitches I seem to remember asking the woman next to me if she would slide her chair over a little so I could get my needle back up again!

Several years later, Ida put her arm around me and told me that after I left that first day they picked out every single one of my stitches. I don't know what they did about the blood.

As it turned out my ignorance and naiveté paid off; it certainly wasn't my skill with a quilting needle. I visited with my new Amish friends many times and learned about Amish culture by participating in it. I wore Amish dresses, ate Amish food, and learned to say a handful of phrases in Pennsylvania Dutch. One phrase which got a lot of use was "Nay danky, ich bin urshtum gooka." ("No thanks, I'm just looking.")

I learned to milk cows, hitch up and drive a buggy, and fasten my dress with straight pins. I also husked corn, helped butcher, and attended my first leaf-raking frolic. This was, coincidentally, my last leaf-raking frolic as it reminded me entirely too much of that broom-making thing I mentioned earlier.

My thesis was long and dull and heavily footnoted, but a big hit none-the-less. I passed with honors. Mercifully, a sample of my quilting did not have to accompany the text. Shortly after graduation I announced that I would make a quilt of my own. Ida volunteered to help and the rest, as they say, is history. I have been making quilts ever since.

Unlike other creative endeavors I have experimented with, quilt-making has held my interest for almost 20 years. I'm still not "ahead of the game" as I'll have to live to be 117 to use up the fabric I've already purchased, but I'm having loads of fun. Quilt #73 is partially quilted, #74 is half pieced, and #75 is a pile of fabric on the floor in the corner of my studio. At the end of the book, I'll give you an update.

Meanwhile, should you ever care to go ribbon-less at the next quilt show, let me share some of my beginning quilts with you.

LESSON ONE:
If Nothing Falls Off You're Doing OK

My first quilt came off the cover of a craft magazine. I should have left it there. Instead of templates, piecing diagrams, and pages of instructions, this magazine had little patches drawn on miniature graph paper next to 12 words of "how-to." It was all the way in the back of the magazine sandwiched between ads for hearing aids and support hose.

The reader was supposed to enlarge it. Now there's a concept. You make a bunch of big squares that look like their little squares and re-draw their lines on your paper. Not very accurate. I once made a pair of pants using one of these enlarge-it-yourself patterns and by the time I was finished it had three legs and a lapel!

My quilt pattern was called Converging Blocks and it looked a little like bargello, if you squinted your eyes and stepped way back. Like Montana. The magazine featured it in shades of brown. I went way out on the creativity limb and made mine in blues.

I had a surprisingly easy time of it. The pieces went together perfectly. Remember, I had only really seen three real quilts in my life: the two made out of recycled pajamas and boxer shorts, and the trampoline the Amish women were sewing on. I wasn't that concerned with corners meeting and seams lying flat. When I came to the end of a row I just whacked off whatever hung off or took a pleat. I figured if I shook the top and nothing fell off I was doing pretty good!

LESSON TWO:
Make Bigger Stitches; It Takes Less Time

My Amish friend, Ida, ever the patient teacher, encouraged me. She looked at my efforts, crossed her fingers behind her back, and told me I was doing just fine. When my quilt top was ready to quilt she was there with a handful of her friends and relatives to help.

We put the quilt in frame and quilted as far as we could reach all the way around the outside before the day was over. Those Amish ladies were good, but I was much faster. You can be faster when your stitches are an inch and a half longer than anyone else's.

Such fine stitches. And without a thimble, too.

We rolled the quilt up on the long stretcher bars of the frame, wrapped newspaper around it, tied a red flag to the end, and jammed it in my Chevette for the drive home. Back at school I set up a makeshift quilting frame and injured my fingers in between a full class load, a part-time job, and pestering the poor guy I would eventually marry who lived halfway across the state.

I know. I said that I graduated back there in the introduction. I really did. It's just that after earning a degree in anthropology I came to the startling realization that there is nothing one can do with a degree in anthropology except teach other people how to anthropologize. I went back to school to get a teaching certificate. This at a time when the only openings in Michigan schools were doors and windows.

A short time before the quilt was actually finished I gave it to my parents for their 30th wedding anniversary, starting the beloved and practical tradition of giving quilts not entirely finished. It's much less stressful. I figured Mom could sew on the binding herself.

My parents loved the quilt, but then again I'm an only child. They really were so proud of me. And rightly so. I had just about finished a full-size and nearly rectangular quilt in a scant six months. It pays to make big stitches. It goes so much faster.

LESSON THREE:
Bite Off More Than You Can Chew

By the time I began my student teaching some four months later I was ready for another quilt. I had heard somewhere that a young woman about to be married should have a dozen quilts. Finished ones. I have no idea who made this up, but the wedding was less than a year away and I was 12 quilts behind. Time to get cracking!

Besides, I thought if I invested the time and energy to make a quilt, I'd be more inclined to make the bed, and my true nature would be hidden from my husband forever. This actually did work—for about two weeks.

Like most beginning quilters I picked something small and simple: a Lone Star. That's 968 diamonds for those of you who are counting, cut and stitched with precision by a rank beginner. And without pins. It measured 96" x 118" when it was finally finished—at least on two sides. And, no, I didn't trim off any of the points after I joined the diamonds. Seeing as I didn't press the seams I had no idea they were even there!

And they say curved seams are difficult to do on the machine!

LESSON FOUR:
If Something Goes Wrong It Must Be The Pattern

    I student-taught in a small town in southwestern Michigan that was linked to the rest of the world (Kalamazoo) by a highway prone to collecting snow drifts. When it snowed and the wind blew, nobody moved. That winter we had 12 snow days in a row—the worst winter in 20 years. By the time we got back to school we had to wear name tags.

    I spent my snow days purposefully piecing my Lone Star. My student model Singer, a reject from some home-ec class, wheezed and burped on the kitchen table as I stitched. All day long. I fed hundreds of diamonds between the presser foot and the feed dogs, and when I was all done I had this little, itty, bitty, very lonely star that barely touched the edges of the bed. I was shocked.

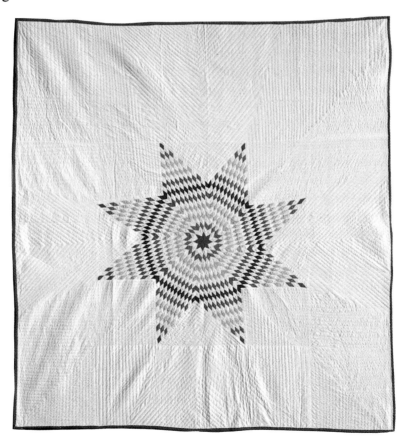

All that work and it didn't look a thing like the grown-up star in the book. And then I realized that the pattern was wrong. The author of the book was a vicious woman who was deliberately out to confuse me and ruin my quilt. Her diamonds were drawn with *double* lines and I picked the wrong line! Cutting on the sewing line wasn't bad enough, didn't she know I had a fat presser foot and my quarter-inch was closer to a third?!

LESSON FIVE:
If It Doesn't Fit, Pull On It Or Cut It Off

As soon as the snow melted I drove down to Indiana to show Ida. She was going to help me "set in" the background and she'd tell me if my star was worth saving. She said we could save it with a little extra fabric. Luckily, the sheet I had bought to "set in" was a full. No skimping here.

I watched my friend stitch and pivot my little star's first point. I was in the presence of greatness. She didn't catch her finger once, and she was using a treadle. I went home to attack the other seven points.

Though lacking expertise, I was brimming with determination. I stretched and flattened the other points into submission. If something didn't quite fit, I just yanked it into place or cut it off.

There's nothing like precision piecing.

LESSON SIX:
Don't Worry, It'll Quilt Out

My top was perfect. It covered an entire bed and then some. I had even gotten used to the puny size of the star. I drove back to Indiana to show Ida, nearly bursting with self-congratulation.

Somehow during the ride down, my magnificent Lone Star became deformed. I don't know if the radio was too loud or there wasn't enough air in the bag, but when we flapped it out on the bed it had a belly big enough to hide a cat. The rest of the quilt wasn't sitting too flat either.

There was way too much quilt around the outside edge and there seemed to be large pockets of air trapped underneath. No sooner did we burp one side than the air pockets re-distributed to an-other! I was devas-tated.

Then I heard those immortal words:

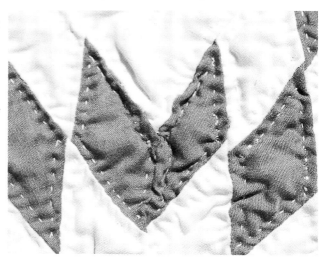

"Don't worry, it'll quilt out."

LESSON SEVEN:
Don't Mark Quilting Lines With Food

The drive back home was filled with hope and resolve. I could not have been more eager to quilt out the four-inch beer belly from the mid-dle of my quilt. Sadly, I was a little too eager. I forgot to mark a quilting design before I put the quilt in frame, only realizing this as I stood before my patchwork trampoline, threaded needle poised and ready. I didn't have a clue where to stick it.

16

Pausing only for a moment, I decided to quilt a quarter-inch around each diamond. Safe move. Then I'd go for something a little more daring in the large open spaces between the star points and in that huge empty area we added to make the quilt fit the bed: echo quilting. I was all set. Now all I had to do was mark the top. Having the quilt stretched in a frame which had eaten my living room was only a minor inconvenience.

I remember reading someplace that the Amish marked quilting lines with a piece of string dredged in flour. Two women each hold one end of the string while a third lifts the string in the center and lets it snap down on the quilt. The resulting *thwack* lays a line of flour in a straight line that will last until it's stitched through.

Two people shy of the required number, I figured I could thumbtack one end of the string to the frame, hold the remaining end with one hand, and pluck the string with the other. As I dragged a hunk of string through the flour I realized that this wasn't going to work. My arms were long enough, but my quilt was white.

Not one to give up, I went back to the cupboard. I tried allspice, cinnamon, and brown sugar before deciding that this was a stupid idea. Frustrated and woozy from the smell of the quilt, I grabbed my yardstick and a #2 pencil. Reaching as far as possible over the *quilt-oline,* I marked fat, dark lines on either side of my yardstick all over the quilt. They were great lines. I could even see them by the light of my three-way bulb and two of its ways were burned out. In fact, I can *still* see the lines.

LESSON EIGHT:
The Faster You Sew On The Binding, The Sooner You'll Be Done

I stitched through the winter and into the spring, finishing my wedding quilt a day before the big event. I had to invent a new way to put on binding in order to save time. It's called the "Jam and Cram Method."

Not wanting to waste precious minutes piecing bias strips together, I cut one long binding snake from the selvage edge, eyeballing the 2½" width. Next I grabbed the quilt, laid the binding on top, jammed it under the presser foot, and hit the gas. I skipped the pins because I was afraid fishing them out of the throat plate after I drove over them would just slow me down. Speed was the key here. Before the quilt fell off the back of the table and moved under its own power, I had to push it through the machine with both hands. When the needle fell off the quilt, I just stopped and crammed the quilt back under. I was done in no time.

I stitched the binding down by hand with my own version of an applique stitch. Never having seen an applique stitch before, I did pretty well. I used quilting thread to stitch down the binding, believing it was illegal to use anything else. I'm particularly fond of the white thread. It shows up so well on the red binding.

Stitching the corners down was my particular specialty. With virtually no practice whatsoever, I was able to master them all: the Pleated, Folded, Whip-stitched, and Mangled Miter. And all on the same quilt!

Four identical corners are just redundant.

Mallery Press, LLC

4206 Sheraton Drive
Flint, Michigan 48532-3557
Phone: 1-800-278-4824 or (810) 733-8743
Fax:(810) 230-1516   MalleryPress@aol.com

TO:

SUSAN SCHMIDT
3317 BROWNLEA CIRCLE
ANTELOPE,   CA   95843

Bill To

SUSAN SCHMIDT
3317 BROWNLEA CIRCLE
ANTELOPE,   CA   95843

Retail Sales Receipt

Date	Invoice #
3/14/2002	34342

Credit Card/Check #	Payment Method	Expiration	Internet Code
-3434	VISA	05-04	YAHOO 1816

Quantity	Description	Price	Amount
1	Picture Play Quilts	22.95	22.95
1	How NOT To Make A Prize-Winning Quilt	8.95	8.95
1	Conversational Mystery Packet (13 fat eighths, assorted)	8.95	8.95
	"I Found The Missing Book" Discount	-1.00	-1.00

AUTOGRAPH BOTH BOOKS

Thank you for your order.

Have a friend? *Get a discount!*
Visit www.AmiSimms.com and "tell a friend"
for a 10% discount when you order $15 or more on-line.
(Follow the link that appears at the bottom of almost every page.)

Subtotal	$44.80
Sales Tax (0.0%)	$0.00
Total:	**$44.80**

LESSON NINE:
Your Husband Won't Mind

Having finished my second quilt it seemed only logical to start the third—on our honeymoon. Technically that's stretching the truth just a bit. After our official honeymoon, we spent an unofficial one at the Simms cabin, now almost deceased. It was a dilapidated old farm house nestled on a lake on the edge of the Huron National Forest, and prior to our arrival it was customary to park the snowmobiles in the living room.

During our first summer of wedded bliss I pieced my Trip Around The World, another full-size over-the-box-springs monster. The fabric had to be purchased in Indiana (six hours each way) for I was certain that quilting fabric could not be purchased in Michigan.

We ate most of our meals on our laps as the sewing machine lived on the table, and Steve learned to find pins with his feet.

LESSON TEN:
Basting Isn't Necessary
If All The Furniture Is Removed

At the end of the summer we moved to Flint. Steve started his second year of teaching and I took up the noble profession of Waiting To Be Called As A Substitute Teacher. This involved getting up very early and lying in bed praying fervently that all the real teachers were still healthy.

Within hours of moving in, the quilt went in the frame. As soon as it did we lost the use of the dining room. It was the only room in the house big enough to accommodate the frame, and it was a tight squeeze even without all the furniture. There were only 6" left over for my chair along one side. To go from the living room to any other part of the house required a drop to all fours. This made it kind of hard to get the phone before the fifth ring, but we managed.

We managed for quite a long time, actually. Back then I didn't know quilts could be basted and rolled. The concept of temporarily sewing the quilt with extra-long stitches so that it could be rolled on the frame (and take up less room) or removed entirely (gasp!) to be stitched on a hoop had never occurred to me. My Amish friends never basted. When everybody got together to quilt they didn't need to baste. The entire quilt was done in a day and a half. Besides, they didn't have to run for the phone.

But, on the bright side, it only took me eight weeks to quilt all the way around the outside edge so that I could finally roll the quilt. By that time we had gotten pretty used to crawling from one room to another under the frame. And it was amusing when company came and asked to use the bathroom.

LESSON ELEVEN:
Mystery Batting

Admittedly I had been a tad eager to start quilting in the new house. Instead of buying name-brand batting in the plastic wrap, I settled for Mystery Batting instead. You know the stuff. It comes on a roll and the clerk at the store has no idea who makes it. It just appears from out of nowhere. If you use it and like it you'll never find it again. If it's rotten, you won't know how to avoid it and there won't be a soul to whom you can complain.

The mystery batting in this quilt disappeared the first time I washed it. Poof! Gone! All I can figure is it must have dissolved in the water like cotton candy. Maybe it got sucked out the seams when the washer hit spin. In any case, it was gone by the time I lifted the lid. I never found a trace. Nothing.

LESSON TWELVE:
Use Sheets For The Back
So You Don't Have To Piece

While cheap batting was not a smart move, I was definitely saving much money in the backing department. Instead of buying real off-the-bolt fabric for the backs of my quilts, I was buying bed sheets. I'm not as dumb as I look. Sheets don't need to be pieced. I could get an entire back out of one king-size sheet. Except that king-size sheets were incredibly expensive, making it cheaper to buy two twins. So I bought two twins and pieced them. Do you get the logic here? Right.

It worked great until I realized that two twins were never quite enough. I always had to go out and buy a third twin (now there's an oxymoron) and piece that on to the other two.

For those readers who have never had the pleasure of quilting on percale, a few pointers. Remove the hems and the piping *first*. It's very hard to do this while the quilt is in frame. The little tag that tells what size sheet you've bought and the sticker personally introducing you to the sheet inspector should probably go, too.

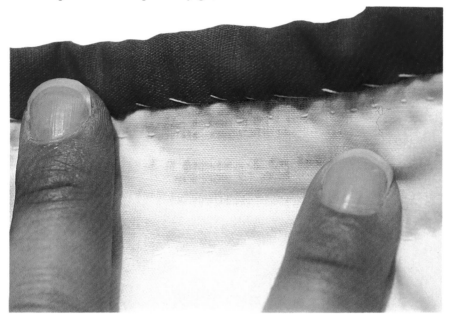

Remove the tag <u>first</u>.

LESSON THIRTEEN:
When Bad Binding Happens To Good People

I got into a little bit of trouble with the binding of my Trip Around The World quilt. (Hard to imagine when I was doing so well.) When I got to the end, I overshot the beginning by several inches. And, for some unknown reason, the tail end of my folded binding strip was a good inch wider than the beginning. Even though I took a pleat when I stitched it down, I still wound up with a little gap.

The choice at that point was very simple. I could either un-sew, or keep a rolled twenty in there for a little mad money. Since the seam ripper is an ugly and potentially dangerous tool, and the little pocket was on my side of the quilt, it was spared.

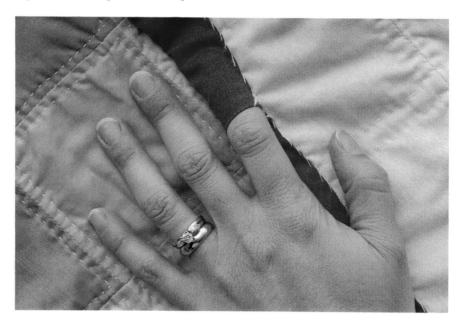

Many people find this binding innovation attractive.

LESSON FOURTEEN:
If You Can't Applique, Paint

With my second bed quilt finished it was time to move on to another challenge. By this time I was gainfully employed on a full-time basis teaching second-graders. Our classroom was in an old building and the door opening onto the hallway had a large window. The principal had an annoying habit of roaming the halls looking in the windows. Obviously the first thing on my agenda was to make a quilt that covered the window.

As you remember from Lesson Eight, my applique stitch had not yet been perfected. Instead of fussing with needle and thread, I went to the craft store and bought what people who cheat at cross-stitch buy to make the little Xs. I carefully drew my pattern on the fabric and *painted* my way to success.

Opting for paint over applique.

The little paint tubes came in loads of different colors, but were obviously made to paint thin, narrow lines. In order to cover the square footage I was interested in, I had to squeeze *really* hard, prying my fingers off the tubes with my leftover hand every time I wanted to change colors. The paint, in such large doses, saturated the fabric and bled onto the TV tray underneath. The orange paint in particular didn't do a whole lot to enhance the fine looks of the plastic imitation wood-grain finish, but I was willing to sacrifice quite a bit for my art.

Admittedly, I got a little carried away with the paint. The quilt is wearing so much paint it's crispy. The wings are painted. The body is painted. The head is painted. In fact, the only thing I didn't paint was the fabric around the eyeballs!

I feared I would have to learn to applique in order to get the butter-fly stuck onto the background fabric. Luckily, before wasting all that time, I hit on an idea that was just as good. I pressed and basted the raw edges of the butterfly under, set him on the black background fabric and basted him in place. Then I layered the background on top of the batting, threw the backing underneath, and *quilted* him down! I skipped that pesky applique part altogether. That's how I was able to get the choppy curves, mangled points, frayed edges, and even longer quilting stitches. No matter, it all seems to go along with the rounded square corners and the pipe-cleaner antennae.

LESSON FIFTEEN:
Creativity Increases When You Run Out Of Beds

Having only one bed and two quilts for it, plus the window quilt, I could have stopped and taken up tole painting or auto repair. But, impas-sioned with quilting as I had become, it was necessary for me to go on.

I remember sitting and thinking one day, what else could I quilt? What surface in my home needed artistic embellishment? Then I looked up and suddenly it hit me. I could make a quilted shower curtain. It was either that or a quilted toilet seat cover: Storm At Sea, or Ocean Waves.

I decided on a pictorial quilt depicting the actual scene were one to pull back the shower curtain. I sat myself down in the hallway, the bath-room being a tad small, and started to sketch. Nothing happened. I had expected my pencil to glide effortlessly over the paper and somehow generate a workable pattern. With seam allowances. In about 20 minutes.

Nothing. I sat there all afternoon but my stupid hand didn't make a single mark on the paper. I switched paper. Maybe graph paper would do the trick. Still nothing, so I put the chair back and started circling ads in the yellow pages under Schools, Auto Repair.

I tried again the next day, having decided that I had not been prop-erly motivated before. I sharpened my pencil, put the graph paper on a clip board, repositioned the chair, and parked a glass of ice water in my non-drawing hand. Refills from the pitcher at my feet were mandatory. If the pencil didn't move, I was to drink.

The idea, of course, was that I was done fooling around. Certified quilt artists like myself aren't supposed to be afraid of making mistakes. It was important just to start and get *something* down on paper. It could always be changed. Meanwhile, I was going to either draw or sit in a puddle.

Long about the time my eyeballs started floating, I had a workable design. Boy, was I relieved! I enlarged my graph paper pattern and lost only one wall in the process. Being so familiar with textile paint, I painted the design on the shampoo bottle. I did a crude, but acceptable, job on the applique. The shark fin was added after I started sewing. (The movie *Jaws* was very popular at the time.)

"Shark In The Shower"

The quilted shower curtain was a huge success, especially when company came. It was visible from the sofa in the living room and people would usually do a double take in mid-sentence which amused me no end. We used the shower curtain (with a liner behind it) for years, until we re-tiled. Sadly, the new tile didn't match the curtain and it was retired. That was probably a good move. The batting had started to shift, and rust stains were beginning to appear on the quilt. Besides, the more I looked at the shower nozzle the more embarrassed I got.

LESSON SIXTEEN:
Orange Is Worse Than Yellow (Trust Me)

Although I've never been too good at figuring out *how much* fabric to buy, picking out *which* fabric to buy had never been a problem. Back then it was pretty simple: get three colors that go together and you're done. This particular quilt troubled me because I'd never gotten such a peculiar reaction from a sales clerk before. When I put the bolts of fabric on the cutting table she asked me if I was "sure." Several times.

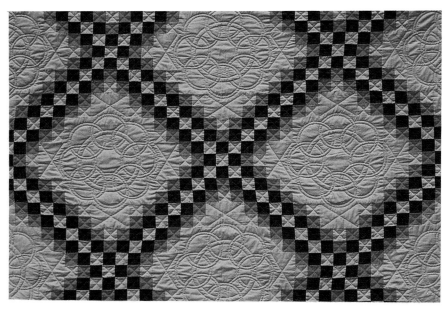

Way too much of good thing.

I had no idea this quilt was going to be so orange. Even when I was piecing it I didn't have a clue. Selective color blindness. That third color, by the way, is brown. If you put that much orange next to brown it turns green! (And you thought yellow was difficult to work with.)

We actually do use this quilt on our bed. Once a year, on Halloween. We don't have to turn on the night light.

LESSON SEVENTEEN:
Pre-washing Isn't Necessary If You Don't Swim

My orange monster won a Certificate of Merit at the local quilt show. I think the judge felt sorry for me having to look at all that orange. Her only criticism was of my quilting.

Like most quilters, I didn't particularly enjoy going through seam allowances. My needles bent, my fingers hurt, and my stitches got longer. So I just skipped that part. I quilted diagonally through each square like I was supposed to, but when I got to the seam allowance I just slid my needle in between the layers and came up on the other side! It made these cute little fabric bubbles on the back where there should have been longer stitches and blood stains. The judge didn't like it, but I'd probably do it the same way were I ever to make another Irish Chain.

There is just one thing I would have done differently, however. I would have pre-washed the fabric before I chopped it up. Had I run that orange stuff through the washer I would have discovered that it bled like a stuck pig. Instead I threw a wet bathing suit on the bed and dyed the sheets

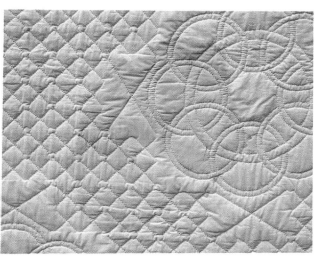

The "Wet Bathing Suit Test" for color-fastness.

underneath, too. The orange fabric still bleeds. I'm not too sure which orange is the culprit, but I've washed that stupid quilt 97 times and the water always looks like carrot juice. Not to worry, the bathing suit stains are colorfast.

LESSON EIGHTEEN:
Reruns Can Be Inspirational

I knew I was getting good when I could tell how other people made their quilts. I could look at a quilt hanging at an exhibit or flapped out for Show & Tell and figure out just how they did it. I could match patch for patch, drafting even the most complicated patterns in my head. I threw around terms like "One-Patch," "Nine-Patch," and "Looks Like Applique To Me" with the best of them.

I knew I had become a true Quiltmaker (with an upper case Q) one afternoon while watching a Mary Tyler Moore Show rerun. In this particular episode Mary was talking to Rhoda, who was in bed trying not to wake her husband, Joe. (I'm sure you remember.) On the bed was a quilt. It was a most magnificent quilt. The colors were extraordinary, the pattern exquisite. It was truly inspired and so was I.

Without wasting a moment I grabbed a pencil and started to sketch. Even though the quilt was on the screen for only a few seconds I was able to draft the pattern and capture its essence. I sketched and erased, and sketched again to get everything just right. I made notations as to size and color. I underlined and outlined and cross-hatched until my pencil was just about down to the wood. I was ready to count blocks and calculate yardage when the quilt blipped off the screen for the last time. Still, I had done it. With what I had, I knew I could make that quilt. I had arrived.

I immediately set out the next day to collect fabric. I couldn't possibly wait for a trip back to Indiana to buy it, so I scoured the local shops. I hit them all, collecting half-yard pieces of the best colors from every dime store within driving distance. Sadly, my local quilt shop was out of sync with my fabric preferences. They foolishly stocked cottons which I wouldn't touch. All that shrinking, wrinkling and fading. I only wanted polyester blends—high-quality fabrics which would wear like cast iron and needle like it, too.

Yes, this was going to be my Master Quilt.

The dreaded four-patch, otherwise known as the MTM Rerun quilt.

LESSON NINETEEN:
If You Want Warmth, Buy An Electric Blanket

Through all of my quiltmaking Steve has been my silent partner. He doesn't help design my quilts, go with me to pick out fabric, or gush and fawn when the quilts are finished. He does, however, encourage me in other more important ways. I get guilt-free teaching and travel time, a partner who does his share of the work plus most of mine, and a really nice guy who never once complained about dropping to all fours to answer the phone.

I was more than a little surprised when he asked me one day if I was going to make any more quilts. Actually, I panicked. My heart started thumping and I broke into a cold sweat. Did this mean he'd had just about enough? Would I have to quit pre-washing my fat quarters with his dress slacks? Was I going to have to find another place besides the trunk of his car to store my overflow? Had he found my stash of fabric between the mattress and the box springs? (The bed *was* getting a little harder to climb into.)

Alas, I need not have worried. He just calmly said that if I was going to keep making quilts, would I please try to make them warmer. I was flabbergasted. And quite relieved. As it happened I had a quilt top all ready to go in the frame—that incredibly sophisticated and highly technical four-patch on the previous page. And if my husband wanted a warm quilt, by golly, I was all too happy to make him one!

I reasoned if one layer of Ultra Fluffy Quilt Batting wasn't warm enough, maybe *two* would be. I found a couple of extra bed sheets that weren't doing anything, and I whipped that puppy in the frame so fast my hair blew. I was on a mission.

Maybe I moved a tad too fast. After about a week of quilting I noticed a couple of things. First, working my needle through all that polyester, the percale sheets, and the double layer of batting was not fun. It was like trying to quilt through a sanitary napkin. And second, I noticed that the lining was a little shy on the south side of the quilt. By about 2". Somehow as it went in frame either the top grew or the sheets shrank, but they no longer met at the edge of the quilt and I was in deep trouble. Personally, I'd like to blame it on the batting.

No amount of yanking did any good. At one point I braced the frame with both feet and tugged at the lining only to pop out half the pins on the far side and break three fingernails. It wouldn't stretch. And there was no way it was going to quilt out.

I didn't want to un-sew all the quilting stitches I had already put in, fix the lining, and put it all back in the frame again. That would have been much too depressing. Instead I moved one of the infamous orange-streaked simulated wood-grain TV trays over to the frame and set my sewing machine on top. Then I un-pinned the offending side of the quilt.

Carefully laying back the top and batting, I moved the TV tray closer to the frame, lifting the machine slightly so that it sat half on the table and half on the frame. Ever so carefully I slid the lining under the presser foot, laid a four-inch strip of leftover sheet underneath it, made sure nobody was looking, and hit the gas.

Even though I was in a big hurry to get on with the quilt, I had to sew slowly. After only about half a foot all the stitches started going in the same hole. The frame didn't look too square anymore and I was afraid of the noise the machine was making. So I stopped, moved the TV tray forward and started again. I sewed like this, inching the machine and the TV tray along the side of the quilt, until I had corrected my little oversight.

The entire venture was most successful. Not only was I able to add more fabric where it was needed, but I also added a third dimension to the quilt—a little pleat in the corner on the back. This was made possible by the extra lining fabric and my careful binding.

Machine stitching "in the frame" adds dimension.

LESSON TWENTY:
Don't Add Seam Allowance More Than Once

Early on in my quilting career I bought my first pair of Gingher scissors. I bought them because the man at the fabric store used them to cut through eight layers of polyester-blend fabric at once. I couldn't give him my money fast enough.

I was so excited I took the scissors home and cut out two full-size tops that very evening, eight layers at once. I set the speed record for slicing polyester. The scissors worked like a charm. I could cut without working my mouth and I didn't grow a blister on the side of my pinkie.

Sadly, when I started sewing one of the tops, I realized something was a little off. Things just weren't fitting together real well. Possibly my chalk pencil needed sharpening after 427 successive tracings, or maybe I dragged it around the cardboard a little too fast. The eight layers of polyester couldn't *possibly* have shifted as I cut. Nope, it was the templates.

When I cut the cardboard for one of the templates (with my new scissors) I couldn't remember if I had put the seam allowance in or not. So, just to be sure, I added another ¼" all the way around. (I remembered the trouble I had with my Lone Star and I didn't want to make *that* mistake again.)

This was not necessarily a smart move. Every time I got to that one patch, no matter what I sewed it to, I had to e a s e it in with both feet.

LESSON TWENTY-ONE:
Knots Are Nice But Welts Are Better

From the beginning of my quilting career I was taught to bury my knots when starting a thread and to sneak the tails inside the batting when ending. I had no trouble pulling the knots in. A couple good jerks and they either broke off or made a hole in the quilt. And I was always smart enough to pull those suckers in from the top, where I could see what kind of damage was being done, not from the back where it was left to my imagination.

Still, I never felt good about weaving the tails. It seemed so temporary. So I improved the technique, reasoning that if weaving was OK, backstitching would be better. And, if a little backstitching was good, more backstitching was best.

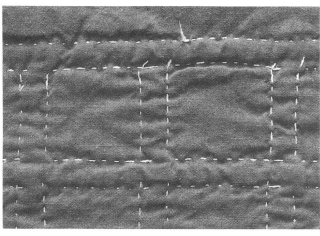

Ending threads for the visually challenged.

LESSON TWENTY-TWO:
People With Big Chests
Shouldn't Quilt In Small Cars

One day my mother announced that she wanted a Double Wedding Ring quilt. As soon as the words were out of her mouth, we both decided it would be best if my Amish friends made it for her. They did and I got the scraps. The leftover blue prints were immediately stitched into a small crib quilt. We had no baby for the quilt, but I, ever the optimist, pieced the top anyway.

A short time later we planned a car trip to see some friends in Kentucky, and being a quilter, I knew the rules. One cannot leave home without piecework in one's purse. Unfortunately the top was already pieced, so my choices were to either sit in the car for 12 hours and look out the window or quilt the top. Easy choice, until I realized I would have to quilt without my frame. Lap quilting was illegal in my county, so I opted to buy a hoop and give that a try.

We hit the quilt shop on the way out of town, but all they had was this 32" oval number. I bought it anyway, fired it up, and ran back to the car. As I jogged to the street, the wind caught the dumb thing and I almost lost it. Steve saw me struggling and came out to help. We wrestled it out of a low branch and I crawled into the Chevette. Then we wedged the hoop in between my chest and the dashboard of the car, a tight squeeze even with the seat pushed all the way back. Steve tucked in whatever leftover fabric wasn't caught in the hoop and, using most of his weight behind the door, managed to close us in.

It was an interesting trip. There was certainly no danger of my hyperventilating. Shallow breathing was hard enough. I didn't have to hold the hoop, either. And it was a lucky thing that I was used to working on a frame and could quilt in all directions, since there was no earthly way to turn that hoop.

I survived the trip and managed to finish most of the quilting even though I lost a spool of thread and at least one bra size. The thread went down the hole behind the hand brake. I wish I knew where the other went.

I'd like to digress for a moment and focus on the back of this particular quilt. It will reinforce a lesson you've already learned. Remember Lesson Twelve about using bed sheets for quilt backs so you don't have to piece? Good, I knew you would.

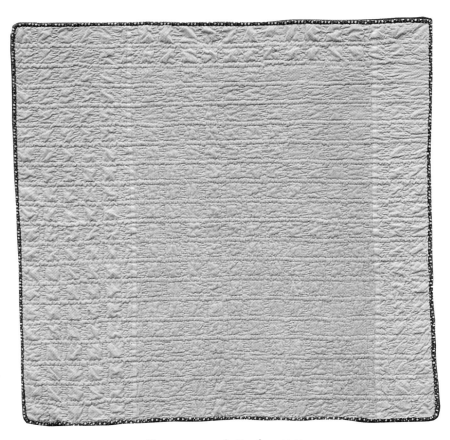

Two seams are better than none.

This quilt only measures 36" square. Notice how many seams I didn't have to sew because I used bed sheets instead of real fabric?

LESSON TWENTY-THREE:
Measure Everything—Even The Bed

Strange as this advice sounds, it can actually save time in the long run. I still seem to have a hard time remembering to measure things, but still, I highly recommend it. The Log Cabin on page 36 is a case in point.

I found the block in a pattern book and made the whole top in a day and a half. That's pretty impressive considering I hadn't yet discovered rotary cutters or quick stripping methods. I was still tracing around ratty looking cardboard templates with dull chalk pencils. It was so much more accurate that way.

I made all 80 blocks just like the ones in the book. More or less. For the first 12 years I quilted, I thought the distance from the side of my presser foot to the needle was ¼". It looked like ¼" but, of course, I never measured. Turned out it wasn't even close, which explains why none of my patchwork ever went together without a fight. Be that as it may, the blocks looked great. Some of them were even *square*. I decided on a barn raising set and stitched them all together.

The day I finish a top I usually flap it out on the bed and sleep under it for one night. It's a good luck thing. The Quilt Fairies come while I sleep and fix all the bad seams. The afternoon I finished this quilt, I spread it out on the bed and just about had a hemorrhage. This thing was huge. It covered the top of the bed, went down the sides, and was on its way to the bathroom!

I was at a loss as to what to do. Obviously the mattress, box springs, and bed frame must have been *irregulars*. I had no idea. Stuck with an odd-size bed, I had to fix the quilt. It needed to lose an entire row off one side and another row off the bottom to have it come close to being the right size. But I couldn't just whack off those extra blocks—the quilt would no longer be symmetrical. I'd never be able to sleep under it.

Thankfully, after a good 15 minutes of hard thinking I had it all figured out. First I made the bed. Then I centered the top on the bed and smoothed it all out very carefully. I took my Ginghers and, on hands and knees, trimmed the quilt to fit the bed!

Trimming the quilt to size was a stroke of genius. I chopped off two logs on the right side, whacked off a log and three quarters on the left side, and sliced right through the middle of the chimneys on the bottom. It was a little hard going around the pillows, but I managed.

The top looked great and finally fit my deformed bed. It went in frame the next day, and it wasn't until I held the quilt up in front of a group of quilters and someone remarked about the partial blocks and skinny logs that I realized this may not have been the best way to re-size the quilt.

No matter. My Log Cabin quilt has been living on our bed for years and unless visitors walk all the way around the bed staring at the binding, this slight imperfection is never noticed.

Measure the bed *first.*

Real Women Don't Split Floss

Shortly after making the Log Cabin, I bought another quilting book. I was probably up to several dozen by this time, but I had never actually read any of them. I'd buy them, and just look at the pictures. I now realized that reading the text can add quite a lot.

The book I bought was Jinny Beyer's *Patchwork Patterns*. (If you already have all of *my* books, you should run right out and buy hers.)

I figured as long as I was making all these patterns I should make blocks to go with them and make a Sampler Quilt. I hadn't done one of those yet and they appeared to be all the rage. So, I went and bought two coordinating prints and a solid, all brown. That was exciting.

The quilt took longer to make than I thought it would. By the time the top was together I was starting to forget the names of the blocks. Terrified that someone would ask me what they were called, I embroidered the names of each block on the sashing strips below them.

Embroider the names of hard-to-remember blocks so you won't forget.

Unfortunately I didn't know as much about embroidery as I did about quilting. I knew that the knots went on the back and after that I started to flounder. Some things I just had to figure out on my own.

Floss, for example, is sold with six threads all together. I reasoned that if that's how they sold it, that's how they wanted me to use it. So I did—six strands at once. It was like sewing with rope. I had to use pliers on just about every stitch and every time I yanked the eye through the fabric it made a nasty sound.

LESSON TWENTY-FIVE:
Only Sissies Machine Quilt

Shortly after the Brown Sampler came off the frame I was laid off. The school system claimed they had run out of second-graders. So, through no fault of my own I drifted into full-time quilting. Thankfully, by this time I had also hung around the quilting world long enough to learn certain basic truths, which prepared me well for my new vocation.

One such truth is that machine quilting is not as good as hand quilting. If it were, it would take longer and hurt more. Machine quilters count hours not months and their fingers don't bleed. This just isn't fair. Machine quilters give quilts as gifts without promissory notes. Their quilts are finished *before* the day they are given. This isn't fair either. My daughter is expecting a high school graduation quilt. I know this because she has been dropping hints. She's only eleven. She knows. Even with advance planning I'm never going to make it. She's *got* to go to college; I need the extra four years.

I have a friend who works full time, teaches quilting classes at three shops, has a husband and two kids, and in the past three years has made over 80 quilts! All on the machine. In the time it took to type this, she probably finished another one. If the Quilt Police were on the ball, this woman would have had to surrender her even-feed foot long ago.

It's also widely acknowledged that machine quilting is not as good as hand quilting because there is virtually no skill involved. The machine, obviously, does all the work. Hence the name: machine quilting.

Using the even-feed foot is a no-brainer. The hardest part is getting the foot on. (Take the other one off first.) It doesn't take a rocket scientist to free-motion quilt either. Drop the feed dogs, put a brick on the foot pedal, and swish the quilt back and forth. There's nothing to it.

Still, for whatever perverse reason, I wanted to try machine quilting anyway. I had a small medallion quilt top with a Rail Fence center. It was too small for a bed and too large for anything else. And, I didn't like it well enough to hand quilt. Perfect. I marked the quilting design, pin-basted with those annoying little brass safety pins, and dragged it over to the machine. It took me three quarters of an hour to attach the even-feed foot, unscrewing half the machine in the process.

Starting at the outside border I soon discovered there must be some trick to this after all. Things weren't going too smoothly. I totally wrecked the first border by driving off the marked lines and over the little brass safety pins. It's hard trying to stuff an armful of quilt the size of a sleeping bag through that small whole between the needle and rest of the machine. Incidentally, those safety pins are awfully hard to get out of the throat plate. Once they go down, they don't come up without a fight. There was too much damage to save the border so I whipped out my scissors and cut it off.

I began again on the "new" outside border. This one would be much easier; I was all warmed up. The cable motif, however, proved even more difficult. Not only was it harder to steer, but little pleats came out of no-where. There was also something wrong with the back of the quilt. After a few inches of quilting it would slide right off the table. I'd reposition it and, as if the back had turned to Teflon, the slightest movement would send it over the edge again. When the quilt wasn't sliding, the little brass safety pins were catching on the front lip of the table. Oddly enough I never realized this had happened until I'd planted 6" of stitches in 1½" of quilt. I chopped that border off, too.

There must have been something wrong with my even-feed foot since it couldn't follow the quilting lines I had marked, so I yanked it off the machine and elected to free-motion the feathers on the next border. With two less borders the quilt would be easier to maneuver, and in its reduced size it probably would stay on the table for longer periods of time. I was ready for success.

I slid the quilt under the needle, held my breath, and hit the gas. My hands firmly positioned on either side of the needle I attempted to coax the quilt back and forth. Nothing. I dug in my fingernails and lowered my elbows to help move it and it still refused to budge. The needle was going full tilt, depositing stitches in a huge welt that looked like a but-tonhole with a glandular problem. I couldn't get that stupid quilt to move more than ½" in either direction. Possibly this was because I had forgot-ten to drop the feed dogs. Off came the border.

This was my last chance. If I failed here, my shrinking quilt would be borderless. I dropped the feed dogs, leaned way over, and positioned as much of my arms on the quilt as possible to help push. I looked just like Richard Nixon doing a victory salute. No danger of catching my fingers in the needle; I was looking at a forehead injury. Ready for just about anything, I stomped on the gas and began flailing my arms. Whoa, Nellie! That quilt started to slip-slide all over the place! I had big stitches; I had little stitches. In less than 10 seconds they were all over the quilt, running in every direction from my finger tips to my armpits. Luckily I kept all of my body parts clear of the needle and was able to take my foot off the gas and sit up before sewing my face. My hands still shaking, I cut off the last border.

Staring at something decidedly smaller than what I started with, I re-attached the even-feed foot and aimed the needle at what was left of my quilt. Barely touching the go pedal, I stitched very *s l o w l y*, dropping the needle down the middle of each fence rail. I could probably have hand quilted it faster.

This is all that was left of my medallion quilt.

LESSON TWENTY-SIX:
After 53 Quilts You Can Still Make A Dog

Despite my questionable success at machine quilting I did try it again. Like the other quilts I've described so far, I was just too stupid to give up. I really liked making quilts. Even from the beginning I never thought I would just make one quilt and stop. Since none of my quilts blew up, melted, broke, or unraveled, I was far more successful with quilting than I had been with anything else I had ever tried. Besides, I thought my quilts were terrific.

When I first began, my Amish friend, Ida, was the only other quilter I knew. Every time I finished a top I'd drive it down to Indiana to show her. She'd tell me it was really nice and I'd go home and quilt it. Then I'd make her look at it again when it was finished and bask in the praise that I always knew would come. Her enthusiasm and support never wavered. She never groaned, rolled her eyes, or ran from the room covering her mouth. She always gave me the confidence to make the next quilt.

When I finally started meeting other quilters and seeing other quilts I realized what a non-threatening start I had enjoyed. I also realized there was more than a little room for improvement. Thankfully, by that time I was also pretty cocky. Finding out I was totally inept didn't flatten my self-esteem. Instead, I started learning from other quilters, reading quilting books and magazines, and scrutinizing quilts at shows. I even entered a few quilt shows myself and actually came to embrace a lot of what that lunatic in the white gloves had told me years before!

Having something to shoot for, be it smaller quilting stitches, matching points, flat seams, or hidden knots was a good thing. I became a better quilter.

Things didn't change overnight; improvement came in short steps. I don't embrace change without a pretty good reason. I was well into my second quilt, for example, before Ida convinced me to use a thimble. Prior to that, not only was I making hamburger out of my bottom finger, I was continually ramming the eye of the needle through the one on top! I also started using #10 betweens when the embroidery needle I found in the junk drawer in the kitchen finally broke. I had no idea that needles came in sizes!

I finally got my hands on a decent sewing machine, too, after only five years of quiltmaking. That was a pleasant change. I traded the old student model in for my first Bernina. It was either that or take the old clunker back up to the Simms' cabin, tie it to the end of a long rope, and use it as a boat anchor. Still, it really did take me 12 years to make a true ¼" seam. I just never got around to actually measuring the distance between the needle and the side of my presser foot until then. Deep in my heart I knew my seams were probably a little off, but being a mathematical incompetent, I thought it would be OK as long as I was *consistent*. (It doesn't work that way!) And please don't tell anyone, but I didn't learn how to use a rotary cutter until 1990!

Still, in spite of my backwards tendencies, I improved. As you might already know, however, quantity does not necessarily ensure quality. With over 50 finished quilts under my belt I was still quite capable of making a dud. While working on a quilt for *Classic Quilts: Patchwork Designs From Ancient Rome*, I realized I had blown it when I liked the back better than the front. (Don't worry, it's not in the book.) I happen to be working on a quilt right now and my favorite part is the *batting*! This could be a problem.

LESSON TWENTY-SEVEN:
They're MY Quilts And I Like Them

We're getting to the end of the book here and it's time to get serious. I've spent the last 40 pages maligning nearly two decades of my quiltmaking, and I don't want you to get the wrong impression. I've enjoyed every quilt I've ever made. Even the rotten ones. The process has always been challenging and fun. I'm more fond of some quilts than others, but that's OK.

It doesn't particularly bother me that it may have taken a tad longer for me to learn to do it "right." After all, who's to say what's *right* and what isn't? Oh-oh! I'm in for it now! Let me explain.

Learning from others who do what you do is terrific. By all means study how other quilters make quilts. Take classes, read books and magazines, get involved with quilt guilds and study groups. Attend quilt shows. *Enter* quilt shows. Feedback from others can be a great learning tool, especially when the "expert" knows one end of a needle from the other. You've got to make sure, however, that the advice the expert is giving makes sense to you.

Let me give you an example. After I had made about 10 quilts, I started entering quilt shows. I only entered shows which gave written critiques. I wanted to know what the judges thought of my work. (I also hid behind my quilts at the show, pretending I was looking at something else, so I could hear what "real" people thought, too.) Usually the feedback made sense and helped me do something better. If a judge wrote that I could improve my piecing, for example, I felt awful for a few hours and then tried to get my corners closer. The advice made sense to me. I'd seen quilts with matching points and it was something I wanted to emulate. One judge, however, wrote that the quilting thread I'd used on one of my quilts didn't match the *back* of the quilt. That was just about the stupidest thing I'd ever heard of! Who in their right mind cares if the thread matches the *back*? It should match the *front*.

Sometimes judges are misinformed; sometimes they're just wrong. That terrible orange Irish Chain quilt on page 26 may have its faults, but in my opinion the quilting strategy (sliding under the seam allowances and coming up on the other side) isn't one of them. The judge and I just didn't see eye to eye. Since it's *my* quilt, the judge was wrong. The moral here is that you've got to follow your own path, even if you're the only one on it.

There are also times, believe it or not, when the value of a quilt is neither in the workmanship nor in the design, but in the life the quilt takes on after it's finished. I had made a quilt early on, using the scraps from several other projects. It was ugly from the start, never got any better, and I couldn't care less. It's one of my all-time favorite quilts.

Using my best 2" square cardboard template (it was only showing wear on *one* side) I cut patches from just about every leftover I had in the scrap bucket, no matter what the color—even the orange. I stopped when I had filled a grocery sack halfway to the top. I stirred them up, fished them out with my eyes closed, and stitched them together until I ran out of patches. It was too small for anything useful, and I was way too lazy to start cutting squares again, so I added borders. I cut and stitched the borders with the same gleeful abandon as I had pieced the inside, paying absolutely no attention to color, size, or grainline. It grew to crib size and I gave up. The borders wobbled and puckered so severely you could drive a steam roller over it and it still wouldn't lie flat! I named it the "Horrible Scrap Quilt," and I stuck it on the top shelf in the closet. It was even too ugly to give away.

Several years later, we adopted our daughter from Korea. She arrived at Detroit Metro Airport three days before Christmas. There are "greeters" who meet the baby flights. These are people who have also adopted foreign-born children. They go onto the airplane after all the other passengers have left. They change the babies' diapers, comb their hair, change their clothes, carry them off the plane, and then present them to the waiting parents. The night before Jennie arrived the greeter phoned us and went over the procedure. There would be five babies on Jennie's flight and three greeters. When I asked how the waiting parents would know which child was theirs as he or she came off the plane, she told me not to worry, they would find us! Before we hung up, she told us to send an extra blanket onto the plane because it would be cold on the jetway.

I kept worrying that the airport would be mobbed and the greeter would lose us in the crowd. Or, worse yet, they'd hand over our kid to the wrong set of parents! I wanted to make sure we knew the moment our baby came off that plane so we could rush to the end of the jetway for the hand-off. When we got to the airport it was packed with holiday travelers. I gave the greeter the "extra blanket" she'd asked for and tried to hold our place near the gate. It was the "Horrible Scrap Quilt" and thanks to that ugly little quilt we were able to spot our Jennie from a good 50 yards away!

Ugly is in the eye of the beholder.

This brings us to the most important part of the book. It just might be worth highlighting with one of those fluorescent yellow markers. Here it is: *The ultimate measure of your quiltmaking success is not what anyone else thinks of your quilt, but rather what YOU think of it.* Was it fun to make? Are you proud of yourself? Do you get a thrill every time you look at it? Answer "yes" to any of these questions and I don't care what anybody says—you're a winner in *my* book! To prove it, I've got a little present for you. Send a <u>long</u> self-addressed stamped envelope (or international postal reply coupon if you live outside the USA) to:

> WINNER—Mallery Press
> 4206 Sheraton Drive
> Flint, Michigan 48532 USA

∂⍶⍾

Darn. That was my big finish and I seem to have several pages leftover. I probably should have measured something. No matter. Would you like to see my studio? This has absolutely nothing to do with the book, other than that's the place where I'm sitting right now writing this. I thought you might just be curious to see what it looks like. (If you're not, you can read the introduction again and by the time you're through we'll be done here and you can close the book.)

In real life my studio never looks this clean. I had to clean it up because the police came. Not the Quilt Police, the other kind. You see I stack things in piles. Lots of piles. They're all over the floor, on the cutting table, and in the closet. If I need to get at something, I just move the piles around. Sometimes the piles grow to be quite high.

When I'm not looking the piles ooze out into the hallway and leak into the rest of the house. The ones on the floor (especially in the living room) really drive Steve nuts. He says things on the floor are often perceived by others as trash. I tell him his piles on the floor may be trash, but my piles are Important Stuff. This is one of the few things we disagree on.

Several weeks ago the piles got a little out of hand. One of them fell over and set off the motion detector on the burglar alarm. I came home after delivering Jennie to school and found two squad cars in the driveway. The cops were looking in the windows when I drove up. They told me that none of the windows or doors had been tampered with, but they still couldn't be sure if we had been burglarized or not. He gestured to the big picture window in the family room through which I could see piles of Important Stuff. I explained that things looked OK to me. Really.

I tried explaining some more by telling them that I was a quilter. I had to repeat myself twice. Then he wanted to see my ID. As the two of them walked back to their squad cars I overheard one say to the other, "I hope to h _ _ _ *my* wife never takes up quilting!"

This is my fabric stash. As you can see, I don't have enough. I should probably go out and buy more.

I also keep quilting stuff in the basement, the garage, under the bed upstairs, and in the oven. (I just have to remember to take it out before I preheat. Otherwise I'll meet the firemen, too.)

Steve thinks the new pole barn will be for *him.*

This little tour wouldn't be complete without showing you my clothes chute. I don't ordinarily share this with readers, but I see we still have some space left. (I wonder how the others are doing on the Introduction.) Ours is probably the first quilted clothes chute on the block. I made it myself.

It starts in the upstairs linen closet...

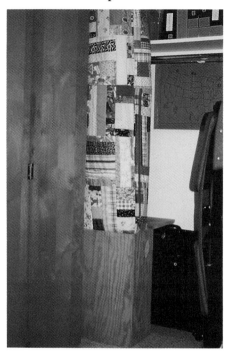

...and continues down through the closet in my studio.

There's a two-foot-long zipper in this section so I can park my garment bag in the closet after a teaching trip and stuff in what needs to be washed right there.

The chute continues down...

...into the basement where it unzips at rafter level. It's a little over 13 feet long from top to bottom and I try never to do the laundry until it's full!

I'm currently working on another system to shoot the clean clothes back up-stairs. It involves several wheels, a couple of pul-leys, lots of rope, and a quilted catapult.

Update

Well, we're done now. Here's the update I promised on page 10.

In the time it took you to read this book, I finished quilt #73, #74 is ready to baste, and #75 is still sitting in a pile on the floor in my studio. Not bad. Still, I'd appreciate it if you would read the book again just once more. That way while you're reading maybe I'll be able to quilt #74, cut out #75, and assemble fabric for #76.

I was just thinking. If you were to buy a copy of this book for a friend and have them read it, then I'd have even *more* time to quilt, wouldn't I? Just a thought.

Other books by Ami Simms

Classic Quilts: Patchwork Designs From Ancient Rome
Creating Scrapbook Quilts
Every Trick In The Book
How To Improve Your Quilting Stitch
Invisible Applique

For a free brochure describing Ami's books, or information about lectures and workshops, write or call:

Mallery Press
4206 Sheraton Drive
Flint, Michigan 48532
1-800-A-STITCH
(1-800-278-4824)
or
(810) 733-8743